never iron when you are naked

Trevor Perry

The Author

Trevor Perry has been speaking about technical subjects to the computer industry for many years. It took him some time to realize he had even more to say, but that did not hold him back. His motivational speaking career began with a session titled *Get A Life!* – this remains his most popular and most requested topic.

Trevor has provided additional information and updates on his website: www.urxo.com

You can contact him at: trevor@urxo.com

Never Iron When You Are Naked .
Copyright © 2007 Trevor Perry . All rights reserved.
ISBN 978-0-6151-4568-6
Images copyright © iStockphoto.com
Portrait photo by Christopher Mann© . Dallas TX
Set in Adobe Jenson Pro
Design and finished art . Peter Holmes . Melbourne . Australia
peter@iguanadesign.com.au

"There is a love in me raging
Alegria
A joyous, magical feeling"

Cirque du Soleil

Introduction

Trevor believes that everyone is on a lifelong search for something – call it destiny, nirvana. He believes while we are on that journey, we cross paths with other people – some for a short time, some for a lifetime – all of whom have an impact. In this book, you will find ideas, stories, and advice, and the lessons learned by someone who discovered a gift for story telling.

Get a Life!

In *Get A Life!*, Trevor works with the audience to adjust their perspective – on life, on living, and balancing all the wonderful things in their lives. He checks everyone's **I-Sight** (that is, their personal perspective), and prescribes **I-Drops** – techniques to help improve **I-Sight**.

I-Drops

I-Drops are 'All The Advice Your Mother Should Have Given You, But Never Did'. Each **I-Drop** is an observation on life from Trevor's own unique experiences and perspective. If you have seen *Get A Life!*, **I-Drops** will be familiar. If not, this book is your introduction.

never iron when you are naked

This **I-Drop** demonstrates why all **I-Drops** are known as 'All The Advice Your Mother Should Have Given You, But Never Did.'

My mother taught me how to iron, and how to iron well. It was one of many life lessons that would provide me with a future of impressing dates and one of never wearing wrinkled clothing.

However, mum forgot to teach me one vital step in the ironing process. To demonstrate, your participation is required. First, stand up, and place your right hand horizontally in front of your belt region.

When you read the word 'here' in the upcoming sentence, wave your right hand in a motion that recognizes that position.

Stand.

Read:

"My mum forgot to tell me that when I grew up, I would reach to 6 feet, 1 inch tall, and that the ironing board would reach to right about *'here'*".

Never iron, when you are naked…

live

When you wake in the morning, do you consciously recognize that you are alive? Or, do you go about the normal habits that require you to simply exist without another thought?

How is your morning coffee? Is it just a starter? Or is it an experience of flavor to be savored – the result of a slowly brewed collection of carefully roasted beans that were grown in the shade on a mountain in the Andes tended by a descendant of the aboriginal population who bargained with Cortez for their gold?

Life is full of many wonders, and you could see them all around you – if you were to look. The smell of rain. A rose blooming. The fluffy rabbit shaped cloud high in the atmosphere. Revel in these wonders.

It is your choice to live within the borders of mundane, or to live a rich life full of the wonders around you.

Live.

Embrace your life!

live passionately

Now that you are living your new life, there are new levels to which you can aspire. Passion is an emotion – powerful and compelling. Living passionately requires a commitment of powerful emotion.

Remember when you were young and discovered something for the first time? Maybe it was the concept of getting a new pet. Or, a toy you wanted for your birthday? The youthful desire for that particular item may have faded, but that passion remains in you – dormant. Mostly.

When life throws new opportunities your way, seize them with a vengeance! Become newly excited about everyday things, and enjoy them with powerful emotion. Find joy in your daily experiences, adding richness and passion to your full life.

Live.

Loud!

love

I took an evening class when I lived in Austin called "Charisma".

The instructor asked us to list the top ten joys in our lives and write them down. The concept was to have this list available when we were sad or feeling down, so we could indulge in one of those joys.

I listed my number two joy as a Caramel Macchiato – something that I could enjoy in many places on the planet. Depending on how low I was feeling, I had to switch to non-fat lattes to avoid the weight gain.

My number one joy was the moment when my daughter told me she loved me – unsolicited. While I could not recreate this moment on demand, identifying that as a joy in my life was a turning point. It was then I understood the meaning of unconditional love, and its impact on my life.

It seems that we often fall into the rut of normalcy, and take life and love for granted. Take time in each day to remember those you love, breathe in and feel that love. In a shorter time than you can imagine, love invades your soul and all conditions disappear.

Love.

Unconditionally!

love passionately

A famous Souza quote, often misattributed to several other sources, contains the line:

"Love as though you have never been hurt before".

I find this particular saying to be a cliché. Some people need cliché to aid their daily lives, and the intent of this particular one is admirable.

Take a different look, and this quote can be revisited, while losing none of its original intent. My personal version is:

"Love so you can be hurt".

When we were teenagers and had our first crush, we did not know what love was. Now we have the experience of love in our life, now we understand the true concept of love, why would we go back to loving like we had never been hurt.

Naiveté, lacking in knowledge, misunderstanding emotion and feeling – these are the things that place us where we have never been hurt. The pain of love has allowed us to know how strong love can be – how passionately we can give of ourselves. Loving passionately, loving so you can be hurt – this is the only way our love will be real, have the depth of truth, and be as rich as it can.

Risk your heart.

You will have love.

fix things now

When my dad was diagnosed with terminal cancer, several friends told me to "fix things now." That surprised me, because I did not think there was anything to fix.

I visited my parents five months before my dad succumbed to his cancer. While there were many things still unspoken, I spent quality time with my dad and my brother, and forged new bonds. The last vision in my head of my dad is the one in the rearview mirror as I drove away – he was standing with his arm around my mum, smiling and waving as I left.

When the cancer finally took its last hold, I spoke to my dad regularly on the phone. On his last night in hospital, I talked to him on the phone. I closed with, "I love you, dad." He replied, "I love you, Trev."

My last vision of my dad and my last words with him are cherished memories. Had there been unfixed things between us, I would not have those memories to treasure.

Recently, a car accident totaled my car. While my daughter and I were OK, I received several notes telling me how people were glad I was in their life. While I appreciate them all, had the accident been my last, those words would have been too late.

Fix things now.

Tomorrow is not a guarantee.

go fly a kite

When I first arrived in the US, someone told me to "go fly a kite". I was standing out in a field, flying the kite, when I realized that was not what they meant!

Have you flown a kite recently? It takes you to a place where you get to be outside, experiencing the weather, and playing with the elements. What an exhilarating feeling of freedom and nature – not something found in front of the TV.

Making your own is an even more rewarding experience when you get to play with the results of your own creativity.

Kites come in all shapes, sizes and prices to suit everyone. You can start with a simple diamond kite for hours of fun. Or, if you have a competitive streak, there are sport kites you fly – the first time you are dragged by a kite is something about which you will tell stories.

Versatility, creativity, out in nature, sharing experiences – what more could you wish?

Go.

Fly a kite!

be funny

When I was in school, a teacher asked me, "Are you trying to BE funny?"

I discovered that a 'yes' answer means you get to meet the headmaster in person.

Obviously, there are times when tact is an appropriate skill one should exercise. Since the word 'funny' contains the word 'fun', we should partake when the opportunity arises, and tact deems it available.

The first secret to 'being' funny is not to try too hard. Funnily enough, the main rule of improv is to stop trying. Read funny things. Watch funny movies. Attend funny shows. Hang out with funny people. With all that 'funny' in your life, it will start to rub off on you – soon you, too, will simply 'be' funny.

I have friends who like to pun. Some of them are skilled, while those who are not, tend to be the ones who try too hard.

The second secret to 'being' funny is to draw the tact line in the correct place. Far too many of us have a conservative tact line. If the funny involves something about which you have a particular anti-bias, step over your tact line instead, and laugh out loud. Now, draw a new tact line – one step closer to 'funny'.

Be funny.

You will gather more friends.

play

There are many four-letter words that are considered improper for daily use. 'Play' seems to be one of those words. As adults, we tend to give up things we consider childish, and often, play is considered just that.

In our business lives, play is often considered unprofessional. Yet, successful corporations use forms of play for team-building exercises, employee personal development programs and company outings. Those companies have a working environment that cannot be matched in the typical bureaucracy – one that is more relaxed, where communication is improved, and employees get along. They work well together, because they play well together.

In our personal lives, play is something to bring us together and bring joy to our lives. At an annual family outing, my daughter and I gathered the mothers and grandmothers who were sitting around talking, and engaged them in a version of softball with a plastic ball and bat, trees for bases. Not only was there much laughter and joy, tree-based softball became an annual event. And when they tell family stories, this one is right at the top.

Play.

You will not expect the joy it brings!

smile

Sure, there are clichés about the number of muscles it takes to frown being more than the number of muscles it takes to smile. Regardless, smiling is simply something that our species finds to be positive.

Monkeys bare their teeth in what looks like a smile when they are threatening.

Conversely, humans bare their teeth when they like something or someone.

This causes the sides of the mouth to lift (a positive word on its own), and a smile to be engaged.

Look at children who have never met before. Put them together in a situation where they can play together, and their smiles will transcend all the biases and cultural differences of their parents.

And, with few exceptions, smiling is contagious. With one smile to start them all, the day can only get better for everyone who bares their teeth!

Smile.

It makes people wonder!

laugh

I once experimented with laughter in one of my sessions — I played a laugh soundtrack. While it only lasted a few minutes, by the end of the track, the entire audience was rolling with their own laughter.

Like smiling, laughing is a contagious human disease — one that changes the mood around you in a few short seconds. When you see someone in public laughing out loud, your own rubberneck kicks in and you have to see — first, who is laughing, and second, what the joke was about.

When you do get caught in the laugh, your body is stirred from the inside out. Your funny bone shakes, and the rest of your neurons are jiggled in an excited and happy state. There are many stories of the old adage of laughter being medicine, and there is scientific evidence to the affirmative.

Each morning, start your day with a dose of laughter with your orange juice.

Find the things that make you laugh, and post them in unexpected places — to provoke your own laughter at unexpected moments.

Laugh.

Out loud!

talk to people

While talking to people on planes is not always pleasant, you can learn a lot about the world from someone else's perspective. The new worlds to which you are exposed (translated in my head, at least) contain many stories and much writing fuel!

My favorite experience was sitting next to a man who introduced himself to me with a huge smile. In the course of the flight, we bonded by sharing many stories – I am sure I dated one or two of his girlfriends!

He told me he had fallen through a roof when he was a firefighter, and showed me the scar on his left thumb from that accident. I showed him the scar on my right thumb – we were bookends!

He recounted that in hospital, the nurse said "Mr. Perry…". What?? I stopped him to tell him that was my name.

We discovered his heritage was the Spanish name Pereiro, while my heritage was the English Irish name Perry.

While we were not actually related, we discovered an amazing set of coincidences. These would have never been exposed without that first step of talking to someone else.

Talk to people.

Open your world to new adventure!

look into people's eyes

On a visit to the supermarket, do you have a conversation with the checkout person – without looking into their eyes? Much of our day can be like this – we rush through, not noticing the people with whom we are talking. This human behavior, to me, is a result of having so many people in our immediate world. To establish or assert our own individuality, we become less focused and concerned on others around us.

At some time in our life, many of us were in the position of being unnoticed, while standing right in front of a person focused on something else. Now, we are the less focused, and the people around us are other people. They have lives, goals, dreams, needs, desires, yet we rush past them.

Take a closer look at people around you. Look into their eyes, and see the depth of their soul. For the most part, it will be just a moment of contact – one to connect. Sometimes, your connection will be longer – one to cherish as you connect more often with your fellow humans.

To kick-start your new soul viewing, challenge yourself to remember one thing about each person you meet – the color of his or her eyes.

Look into people's eyes.

Connect.

use a spel check0r

When you move to another country, spelling is not on your mind. When I was 28, I moved from my native country Australia, to the USA. My first challenge was to be understood. My second challenge was to learn how to spell English in a completely new way.

While this has made me overly sensitive to spelling errors, I find it difficult in a business setting to read some of the communication via email or printed documentation. When I am told we might 'loose' the business, I cannot help but think of it becoming promiscuous, rather than lost.

A recent work associate of mine has such poor spelling, grammar, and punctuation, that it requires time to translate before the actual message is understood. Given that most of our work is done with computers, and spell-checkers are built-in or easily installed into word processing and email tools, it seems an ignorant oversight to miss that one vital step and cause everyone else wasted time interpreting.

Ultimately, poor spelling, grammar, and punctuation are signs you do not care, and any credibility you had disappears.

Spell check everything.

It raises your own standards.

dooty dooty doo

There are many silly phrases or sayings, or even words, that can have an impact on a day. One particular day, I was in a blue funk, and discovered the words *dooty dooty doo*.

I giggled, and my day improved.

Finding words that have a sustained positive impact is not an easy task — unless we focus on it. Someone around us may say them, you may see them on a billboard, or you might hear them on TV or radio. They may be written, spoken, or even sung!

Take for example that song sung on *Sesame Street*. It starts with "Sunny Day, sweeping the clouds away" and continues in the same positive manner. Imagine if you were to sing this on your morning commute, it would be stuck in your head all day! And how can your day be bad when you keep singing that it is 'sunny'?

One of my friends and I exchange *dooty dooty doo* text messages on mornings when we are still have not yet found the wonder of the day. It kick-starts our smiles, and we don't look back.

How's your day?

Dooty Dooty Doo!

play in puddles

Working at a renaissance festival as a performer required some fortitude – especially on wet weekends. The first time you are soaked in your costume is an unforgettable experience, and is intensified by the dribble down your spine when you reach total saturation.

The first reaction is to retreat to a safe and dry place; however, it is difficult to continue performing while hidden away from your audience. Once you accept that you will become wet – and remain so – your disposition improves. What started as misery, becomes play. Acceptance changes your expectations and frees you to make the most of the, otherwise miserable, situation.

I have seen performers bloom when they are soaked. The rain brings life, and they wallow in it. Puddles have been stamped, mud has been flung, and I have seen (and yes, experienced) puddle water-skiing.

This is a most simple life lesson. We wander on our journey of life, and when it starts raining, our first instinct is to retreat to a safe and dry place. Go stand out in the rain. Get yourself wet, let it soak you, and then forge on ahead.

Play in puddles.

Get your feet wet.

iiwii

Pronounced 'ee-wee', this acronym stands for:

It Is What It Is.

There are so many things on the planet that can get in our way and ruin a day. The question to be asked is whether you have any impact on the event. There is so much in our lives over which we cannot exert control. If we cannot, we can choose the usual route – to let it bother us. Or we can accept it – determining iiwii.

A common example is travel – the weather changes, our flight is delayed or cancelled, and we cannot make our appointment. If you look at the crowd in an airport under these circumstances, you can see many irate people, screaming for attention. Since you have no control over the weather, raising your anger simply means –you– are more hot and bothered, and you are annoying someone else who most likely cannot change the weather for you. You are still not going to make your appointment.

If you were on the other end of this appointment, would you forgive someone who was delayed by weather?

I bet you would!

IIWII.

If you cannot change it, you cannot change it.

so what?

After ordering a drink, a friend was a little disappointed when it was delivered with an unexpected extra. He exclaimed: "A martini does not have a straw in it!" and proceeded to ask for a replacement. I was confused – could he not have said "so what" and taken the straw out? Or, did the straw somehow pollute the martini beyond drinkability?

There are so many things in our life that are not to our initial expectations or specifications. For most, the quality of the experience is not impacted – just our ego. We can choose to make a fuss, causing grief and disturbance to more than ourselves. Or, we can choose to accept the situation and speak the mantra: "so what?" and move along.

Martini straws are not our only expectation to lower. If someone annoys you in traffic, if someone pushes in front of you in line, if your dinner is not cooked to your exact standards, if your plane is delayed, if someone says something insulting to you, ask yourself this question:

"Does it really impact the quality of my life?"

If the situation is not life threatening, speak the mantra: "so what?" and move along.

So what?

It's no skin off my nose!

oh yeah!

Do you remember that feeling you had earlier today when someone did something to you that annoyed you? Maybe it was when they left their blinker on for miles? Maybe it was when they cut in front of you – driving or walking?

Other people's behavior can impact our day in many ways and we often let this become negative. Ironically, the behavior that annoys us is something that we may have done ourselves. While we ask forgiveness from others, we cannot forgive our own behavior coming from someone else.

The next time you find yourself annoyed at behavior that intrudes upon your comfort zone, perform a self-check. If it was behavior that some time recently, accidentally, not on purpose, inadvertently, unintentionally, you performed of your own accord, remind yourself with the words "oh yeah!" and immediately forgive the perpetrator.

With your new "oh yeah!" approach, you will be surprised at how often you (used to) get bent out of shape for minor blunders of human nature. Eventually, idiosyncrasies will bother you less, and more of your day will be spent appreciating the wonder in your life!

Oh yeah!

–I– did that, too!

stop rushing for elevators

The first thing we do, when we see the doors closing on an elevator or lift, is to start walking faster. This tends to be the natural reaction brought on by the rush of our lives. Modern elevators are plenty and speedy and another will be along within a very short time. Yet, we still rush for the available one.

Take this pause between elevators as an opportunity. We can catch our breath, and then inhale long and deep for a simple relaxation. If we continue rushing, by the time we reach our destination, we have just added a little extra stress to our day.

By breathing deep and taking that elevator pause to calm ourselves, our mood for the rest of the day will be... *elevated*.

If we are already late for a meeting, additional rushing will increase our stress level. Using those few moments to slow down will mean that while we are still late, we arrive at our destination in a much better mood to handle the backlash of our tardiness.

As an interesting aside, when you do stop rushing for the elevator, notice the looks on the faces of the people already inside. Their puzzled looks of confusion will lift your humor reserves, adding to your improved day.

Breathe.

Another elevator is on the way!

teach

Many of my friends are teachers in one form or another. One of the joys I find about teaching, and one they all express, is when the student experiences the light being turned on. That is the *'aha'* moment, when the student "gets it" – when they truly understand.

While it sounds strange, I hear another story from teachers about the moment of their own *'aha'*. Usually this is while they are teaching a concept that may be just a little on the difficult side. After teaching this 'lesson' over and over, and being good at the concept at the big picture level, there is that one moment when it all comes together and makes sense at a molecular level.

It has been said that a consultant or a teacher only needs to be a fraction more educated on a topic than their customers or students. And, while this may be the easy or lazy approach, the majority of teachers tend to learn more about their chosen subject – simply by the nature of teaching. The natural curiosity of human nature is rarely satiated by teaching according to the 'book'.

Ask a teacher when they learn the most, and they will tell you it happens while they are teaching. Find a subject for which you have a passion, teach it, and surprise your own brain!

Teach!

Satisfy your curiosity.

journey

When you are caught up in a book series, waiting for the author to complete the next story can affect the quality of our patience. I was eager for what would happen in book number six, but did not expect the call on that day from a friend. The call was to complain about her sister who had just finished number six, and then called to tell her what happens in the end.

Of course, in telling me this story, she told me what happens in the end. I felt miffed for a moment, until I realized that the joy of the story is not in the destination, but the journey. I read the book, and found the story to be a well-woven adventure, and a pleasure in the reading.

We easily forget that this is a life lesson. Consumers compete fiercely with each other while they gather possessions. People make goals related to dying with the most toys. Our focus becomes getting, or staying, ahead of the neighbors.

Find the balance in your life where you can achieve your goals and support your family – then enjoy the well-woven adventure that is the journey of your life.

Journey.

The destination will take care of itself.

visit nature

I found myself at the Grand Canyon, off the trail, overlooking a steep drop. As I sat marveling in the view, I could hear the wind whistling through the pines, and I could smell the woods around me, while I sat on the pine needle floor of the forest.

I could almost taste nature.

We live in such a concrete world. Our homes become a refuge of civilization where our comfort level is most important. Artificial and man-made objects become familiar and our only surroundings.

How sad.

It appears that civilization is removing the natural from our nature. Flying from Boston, landing in Texas, I heard a group of young girls exclaiming about the fields by the airport – they had never seen 'actual' cows. I know so many people who tell me they will NEVER go camping – "the dirt!", "the cold!", "the lack of amenities!" I attend conferences where the pools are full of pampered tourists, while the beach 100 yards distant is deserted.

What will it take to get you out into nature? Is it not enough that all your senses will be tantalized? Visit nature. Fondle nature.

Touch nature. Wallow in nature. Taste nature. Find a quiet place, and soak it all in.

Visit nature.

Taunt your senses!

don't adopt other people's insecurities

Each of us has our own set of insecurities. Some of us are plagued by them, others have learned how to deal with them and appear to be immune. Just coping with our own is a lifelong task.

Sometimes, our own insecurities lead us to treat other people differently. Our own behavior is flavored by our baggage. Yet, when someone else behaves in this same manner – that is, when their own insecurities flavor their behavior – it becomes easy to adopt theirs to become our own. Don't we already have a fine matching set?

If someone tells us that we are stupid, and you know you are not, why is it we take it personally? Someone else's flavored opinion of our stupidity causes us to be upset? Under similar circumstances, I find it is best to take a breath, place their opinion into the bucket of "other people's issues", and continue without adopting that slam as personal. Count to ten, then keep on counting!

While it surely is best to keep these particular words inside your head, you can defend your level of stupidity with "I guess you would know, since you are an expert on stupidity?"

Many bags look alike.

Check your own before leaving the area.

be sorry...
don't just say
the words

Being around a horde of people when you are out in the real world can be disconcerting. Bumping, pushing, getting in the way, are all annoyances inflicted – upon you, and by you. Usually, when we accidentally bump or push, an "I'm sorry" bursts from our mouth.

I have discovered no one actually MEANS this particular 'sorry'. Next time someone bumps then bursts, look them in the eye and suggest "no you are not!" You will find only a small percentage of people who will take the time to defend their own 'sorry'.

We often burst 'sorry' when we are not even the pained party. When we get on a plane, and the aisle seat is taken, why do we say 'sorry'? For interrupting their sitting position? Think carefully – they were the person who rushed ahead of you, most likely pushing in front, to get on the plane? They certainly should expect to be disturbed by the middle and window passengers.

Of course, it is simple politeness to excuse ourselves, but we apologize. When we are simply being polite, an "excuse me" would work – with a "please" for emphasis. Reserve "sorry" for moments when you truly mean it.

Be sorry...

Mean it.

write HELP
in the sand

At a conference some years back, a bunch of computer weenies from different branches of the same company headed for dinner. On the way, since we were early, we stopped to look at the sea.

Naturally, we decided to skip stones in the tide, and then write HELP in the sand. After all, isn't that what you do when you are at the beach? Even if it is not a deserted island?

What surprised me was that some of our gang would not take off their shoes and stick their toes in the sand. It was such a simple thing, but a desk-jockey life has removed the fun molecule from many people. What an incredible release it is to stick your toes in the sand on a beach. Taking us back to the child in us, it invokes the play in our genes.

For some people, where they live is not always conducive to finding a decent beach. However, there are many ways to connect yourself to that child you suppressed as you "grew up". Take your shoes off – at work! Run barefoot in the snow – quickly. Stand out in the rain longer than you have ever done – until long after the adult in you hits the wall of your comfort zone. Wallow in the sensory pleasure as if it was your very first time!

Take off your shoes!

Get sand in your toes.

roll down
a grassy knoll

Walking between conference venues, I passed a grassy area where several kids were playing in the grass. The small hill afforded them enough slope to gain serious momentum, and roll all the way from top to bottom.

The first words I heard in my head were my mothers – telling me to avoid the grass stains, since I was in my 'good' clothes. This voice was hard to resist. A smaller voice exclaimed that it was such a childish thing to do. That voice was crushed in milliseconds!

It took me some time to remember that my mother did not buy my clothes any more, and that my 'new, improved' detergent would be able to remove the grass stains. I also realized that turning up to a conference session or a business meeting covered in grass blades would create at least two conditions. First, I would be in a more balanced work/play state of mind – and thus would be much more creative and able to contribute. Second, the other patrons of the meeting would have something else to talk about – this disrupting the usual gossip and politicking. There is no doubt that the meeting would be completely different from all those preceding it.

Maybe, it is time to start a new pre-meeting trend for your organization?

Roll in the grass.

They have detergent for those stains!

draw

A friend asked me for a suggestion of an evening class, and I recommended drawing. She scowled at me, and suggested that people would laugh at her. My thought was that they would laugh, since her drawings would be initially skewed and amateurish. However, during the class, she would be gaining new skills, where soon enough, no one would laugh, and everyone would admire.

I forgot that most people are sensitive to ridicule, and laughter mostly appears to be just that. Ironic that adults cannot play (a childlike behavior), but they can run scared (a childish trait).

So, I took a drawing class. The first thing taught was perspective. My initially skewed drawings (with added perspective) transformed into more accurate depictions of the subjects. An interesting life lesson!

I asked another student to share their drawing, and they hesitated. Just as in life, opening up to other human beings can be full of expectation and hesitation.

While I learned a lot about life from my drawing class experience, I finally had to leave when the teacher called my work "very anesthetic" – and no drugs were involved!

Draw.

Apply some perspective!

paint

Get yourself to your nearest art store. Buy some
large tubes of cheap watercolor paint. Add some
large brushes – flat end, round end, pointy. Find the
largest pieces of white paper you can find. At home,
find a large open area and spread out old newspapers
and a pail of water. Place the white paper down in
the middle of the newspaper-covered area. Squirt
(yes, SQUIRT) paint on one of your brushes.

Now, let loose!

Can you remember when you did this in
kindergarten? If you do, you will also remember
how this activity allows you to express yourself. It is
an activity requiring little thought, and lots of play,
and the results will be whatever you say.

Once you discover the freedom of painting, you can
now claim to be an artist! And, imagine the looks
on your friends faces when you present one of your
framed 'paintings' – how can they refuse an 'original'?

The best lesson to learn from painting is to express
yourself in a more open manner. Either, we are
beholden to computers, where we must fit
everything in between the lines. Or, we are beholden
to pens, where we must write straight and legibly.

Painting requires you to work outside the lines!

Paint.

Loosen up!

use your blinker

During my first driving experience in the US, I was only honked at one time. And, that was from a Chicago taxi, so it does not count. On the same adventure, I discovered Americans do not like to use their blinkers.

Since Australians are well trained in blinker use, I thought it was simply lack of education or lack of blinker-use law enforcement. I even thought blinkers might be one of those optional accessories to choose when you are buying a new car.

Air conditioning: yes; Leather seats: yes; Blinkers: no

I soon found out there was a simpler explanation. Blinkers are not used, because they were invented to help someone else. It is worthy of repeating – blinkers were invented to help someone else! Now, re-read…

Once you are at the wheel of your vehicle, surrounded by a ton or so of steel, plastic and rubber, and with a buffer zone of the immediate ten feet around you, why would you think for one moment about the other people sharing the road with you?

This is the question to consider while you are driving. Courtesy is free – are you actively engaged?

Use your blinker.

Someone else's day will be better.

flying

I dig my toes into the soft earth
unfurl my newgrown wings
bend at the knees
lean my face into the prevailing winds
with a gentle push of my toes against the cliff edge
I am soaring
I glide in a large circle
touch down beside you, several yards from the edge
"it's easy" I say
I lift off once more
I take a running start
soon I have gained distance
far from my starting place
the view from this height is spectacular
the clouds invite me to perch for a moment of reflection
I fly alone now
strangely, not lonely
watching the world from my vantage point
discovering new ways to soar
exploring new continents
pondering new scenery
I pluck a feather
hold it high
searching for the right breeze
letting it go to drift only in your direction
to land at your feet
if you hold it to the light at just the right angle
you too
will discover the secret

Trevor Perry

write poetry

I was asked once to write about my poetry reading experiences. I titled the article *"The Effect of Coffee on Poetry"*. My premise was that most, if not all, poetry readings were in coffee shops for a reason. Since I was the only reader with a coffee, it was not for the drink. I did discover that the ambience of a coffee shop suited the reading of poetry.

Most people have not experienced good poetry, or they were forced to read teacher-recommended poems. This usually prevents potential poets from further poetry creativity. To me, that is sad. I have heard horrible poets read, and within their tripe, there is one amazing gem.

Poetry is one art form that really requires no understanding of the rules. While there are defined rules, and writing to conform can be a challenge, putting pencil to paper and spilling your thoughts randomly can result in genius.

So, grab your writing implement, something to write upon, and feed the paper with your words. When it is complete, you can choose to edit or not, but remember — absolutely no one else needs to know! And, when you write that first gem, share. You are now a poet.

ALL poetry is good.

If you wrote it, it is good!

write

Most people think writing requires pen and paper, and for some, that can be a tedious process. The new world of computers gives us additional choices. If you do not want to write a journal on paper, open up a word processor on your computer. Or, find a blogging tool, and spill your words out on to the web. Whiteboards or chalkboards can provide a place to write, albeit larger and dustier!

Writing is an amazing creativity tool. If you have an unresolved issue, writing the words down will get them out of your head. If they do not look the way you want, scratch them and rewrite. If you are on paper, this only requires a stock of pens and a larger bin.

Writing is also an art form with which to express yourself. Describing your adventures may be a little daunting at first. Take that first step to record the events from your perspective, and watch how your writing prowess evolves. Share with no one at all, or self-publish your adventures with photographs – who knows where it may end!

No matter the form, writing is extremely cathartic. Expressing your thoughts and emotions in written form can save you plenty in therapist bills!

Write.

Get those words OUT of your head!

find your
happy trigger

In the noise of a social gathering, one of the stories was the detail that the storyteller applied to making the children's beds every morning. The punch line emphasized how the teller could not be 'happy' until the beds were made, and made to a precise specification.

One person on this planet knows their "happy trigger". They have discovered the task that must be done each day that will allow themselves to be 'happy'.

For the rest of us who are not so pedantic, we must find something that triggers our 'happy'. Just as the 'joy list' offers us an opportunity to be aware of what brings us joy, knowing our happy trigger allows us to know when we have given ourselves permission.

A smile at yourself in the morning ablutions mirror could be yours. Your first latte of the day. The purring of your cat. Clouds. Sunsets. Flowers. Soft slow quiet snow.

Whatever you choose, your awareness of its trigger status will be the key to activation. Certainly, we may discover several triggers, each of which will bestow permission. However you define your triggers, make certain you employ them on a more-than-daily basis.

Find your "happy trigger".

Shoot yourself with happy!

accept your past

After finding myself at the end of a long separation and divorce, I had discovered I was a different person than I had ever expected. I had grown so much as a result of the experience, and upon reviewing, was not sure what to make of the "new" me.

I decided that I would visit the home of my youth, and reconnect the "new" me with the "old" me. I discovered the 26 acres of vineyard had been torn down, and while there were remnants of my history, most of it was now red dirt.

After I returned to my adopted country, I suffered an interesting phenomenon – all of my childhood memories were replaced with a field of red dirt. It was not until I discovered that I was already "whole", that my memories returned. My attempt to reconnect two parts and become whole again was futile! I was already the sum of all my experiences – all of which combined to give me a new strength.

And in order to accept the person that I am today, I had to accept all the good things and all the bad things I had ever done. Each of those experiences taught me something valuable, and accepting them all was an acceptance of who I have become.

Accept your past.

You are the sum of all your experiences!

don't wish... DO!

As a child, we were permitted lots of wishing. A famous song begins "When you wish upon a star....". Wishing is sometimes the best a child can do with their limited resources, however, it really does help with creativity and imagination.

As an adult, we keep wishing. We wish that we could win the lottery. We wish our life was better. We wish so-and-so would stop telling those stories... And while it is nice to have dreams, those should be goals toward which we are working. As an adult, wishing does not get us anywhere.

Now that we have grown, and we are armed with more resources, the wishing can stop, and the DOing can begin. If you would normally wish for something, put plans into place to make sure the wish is fulfilled. Buy a lottery ticket. Be thankful for all you have, find something to enrich your life, and live! Confront so-and-so with a request that they be an adult themselves...

Taking action towards a goal will not guarantee the end result, but your chances will be mightily improved compared to sitting on your behind expressing a wish upon a star.

DO!

Wishing gets you only dreams.

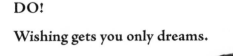

dream

I did not understand the meaning of 'old dog', until I spent time teaching programmers. In a class of fifteen, there were two who were not going to 'get it'. Their blinders were on, their walls were fixed around their small comfort zone, and they were never going to learn any new tricks.

I took it personally, until I realized there are people on this planet who have no dreams. They have found their rut, and it fits the contours of their rear end. These people are the 'old dogs' of the planet.

For the rest of us, dreams are the means to use our imagination to set goals. By imagining what we might want to do in our lives, we open ourselves to new adventures and new worlds. These dreams can add new direction to our lives.

Write down your dreams. Keeping and revisiting a list is essential to fulfillment – it ensures they remain in your subconscious, while teasing them into your conscious mind. It is from here, your dreams will be realized.

Embroider each with fantastical details. The bigger the dream, the bigger the adventure. Dream outrageous. Dream big. Dream things impossible. Dream things not done.

Dream.

Open the door to new adventure.

eliminate omphaloskepsis

Note 1: The Procrastinator's Anonymous meeting is postponed – to be rescheduled. Some time. Soon.

Note 2: The deadline is next week. Hey, I have time! The deadline is tomorrow! I can do it tomorrow. The deadline is today! Er… I think I should start now.

There are moments in my life when I become a bona fide couch potato. My procrastination gene kicks in, and I find some completely non-productive activity in which to indulge. Mostly, these moments tend to be when there is some pressing task that must be done.

Sure, I know I work well under pressure. This claim to fame is a great excuse for sitting on my behind doing absolutely nothing. In the end, though, had I spent that extra time working on my task instead of allowing said behind to grow, there would be benefits.

Quality? With more time to edit or review, the quality of the result could have improved. My reputation for quality work would be enhanced!

Longer life? Pushing the work to the last minute adds stress and anxiety to my life. Surely I can do a better job without stress?

How about you?

Stop watching your belly button.

Get off your behind and DO something!

indulge in omphaloskepsis

Definition: *(n.)* contemplation of one's navel

I worked for a company whose motto was *'work hard, play hard'*. Most of the employees took that to mean *'work hard, party hard'*. While this may seem like balance, intense living between bouts of drinking is not.

From this experience, I discovered a new approach that would work better – *'work smart, play smart'*. The people who took this approach, usually not consciously, seemed to have the balance desired by everyone else.

The 'work' part of the equation is often misunderstood. Working long hours, working when tired or stressed, working under constant pressure, do not constitute 'smart'. Taking breaks to rejuvenate your brain, reenergize your body, and refresh yourself are key to working smart.

The 'play' part of the equation is often misused. Drinking yourself into oblivion may balance the intensity of work, but is not 'smart'. Indulging in your favorite hobby will balance brain, body and soul – sans hangover.

For both 'work' and 'play', taking time for yourself, is smartest. Contemplate your bellybutton, indulge in the relaxation you can find in sorting through the lint.

Find your bellybutton.

Meditate!

stamp out ignorance.
we are stuck
with stupidity

Stupidity appears to be hereditary. Bigotry, prejudice, and chauvinism, on the other hand, while common occurrences in our world, are not based in stupidity, but ignorance.

When a person has not been educated on a particular subject, they will make a choice. The usual response seems to be a denial of that lack of knowledge. This results in further corruption of the truth as they construct their own facts. Normally, this simply becomes a conceited brag. In extreme cases, this becomes hatred for others who do not fit what the ignorant perceive as reality.

The less common choice is to admit a lack of knowledge. This requires humility, honesty, and a stretch of the comfort zone. Once this small step is made, you open yourself to be able to learn. Some of us are lucky to be assembled with the curiosity gene, others need to make a conscious choice to learn.

Once your own ignorance of a subject has begun to wane, it becomes important to stamp out ignorance. It is important, of course, not to push our knowledge on people. Instead, find the opportunities to teach while avoiding the stupid. You too, can change the world.

Stamp out ignorance.

Teach someone something today!

you don't need a policeman

Driving with a friend, a motorist zoomed around us at an extreme speed, and proceeded to weave in and out of the traffic ahead of us. The first words spoken were:

"Where is a policeman when you need one?"

I realized, as it was said, that we did not actually need a policeman. Sure, there was a law broken, but self-appointment as a law enforcement officer did not solve anything. These words were cliché reaction to an event that had nothing to do with us.

Another conversation I had about something I was contemplating concluded with a remark that whatever choice I made, it was sure to result in the best possible result. It took me a moment to realize they had no advice, or simply had some faith in me. Either way, the words were just filling dead space.

We often respond to events in our world, or fill dead space with cliché – in fact, for all the words spoken in a day, it is not hard to imagine that the majority are just filler. The solution seems simple – remove cliché from our vocabulary. However, we might improve our conversations were we to listen more to the others in the conversation – more importantly, to ourselves.

Speak carefully.

Leave more time to hear important words.

collect wonderful memories

I have lived in a different country from my family for over 15 years. After my dad died, my brother, sister, and I have become family again. Of all the amazing results of this catalyst, two stand out.

The first is comparing notes on the memories we have of growing up. While they remember some things that were negative, my personal memory of some of our history is simply not the same. I am not sure if I have purposely forgotten the 'hard times', or if they were really not that 'hard' for me.

What is amazing are the differences in our memories of the same events. Sharing our viewpoints has enabled all of us to see our past with new perspectives. We are finding that the negative parts of those memories are taking on new and positive light. Together we are reconstructing our past, coming to grips with it, and turning it into wonderful memories.

The second result is connecting to each other in a new way. We have become family once more, and our time together has become valuable and precious to all of us. Each time we have the opportunity to be together, we are creating new shared and wonderful memories.

Collect wonderful memories.

Make them first, if you must!

it's not what you have, it's what you show

Having been a performer at renaissance festivals for some years, I became rather oblivious to most of my surroundings while I was performing. It was only when I took a friend, who had never been before, and I was alerted to the amount of cleavage in sight.

While I was focused on entertaining the patrons, cleavage had become part of the scenery. I must admit that when I first arrived, the sheer volume of voluptuousness was noticeable. And thus, the lesson became apparent.

Working as a manager, I have discovered that while some employees have obvious skills to perform their job, it may be a casual conversation that uncovers hidden talents. Had these been visible, that person might have been a greater asset to the company. Are you showing all your talent and skills? If your company cannot see what you can do, they cannot employ those skills.

And like cleavage, revealing a little at a time will continue to pique their interest. Showing it all the time can lessen the impact, and increase the chance of catching cold.

It's what you show.

Show yourself!

write thank you notes

In my mail, I occasionally get a letter or a gift with a thank you note. The boost to my esteem and the recognition of my contribution are high on my joy list. Consider the joy you can add to someone else's day by simply recognizing them or their contribution – with a thank-you note.

Now, inject a different perspective. When someone does something horrible to you, and you recognize your anger or frustration at them, write them a thank-you note.

I was waiting to disembark a plane recently, and I was pushed aside by a passenger in a hurry. Before I calmed down, I found a pen and paper, and wrote these words:

> *"Thank you. Your lack of patience and inability to consider others around you has given me the freedom to test the limits of my own patience and tolerance."*

Not only did this cause me to laugh, my frustration and anger subsided quickly. I screwed the note into a ball and threw it into the trash – with much zeal. I snatched the negative emotions before they could ruin my day, and turned the situation into a positive.

In retrospect, I got my luggage at the same time as I would, had the rude passenger not pushed – and I was laughing to boot.

Write thank you notes.

Be thankful for everything!

observe

I am a self-described coffee connoisseur. My search for the ultimate coffee bean continues with passion. Recently, while riding my motorcycle in my neighborhood, I saw a sign with the word 'Espresso'. On closer investigation, it was a coffee shop! How surprised was I when they told me they had been there about eight months.

Finding a daily routine allows us to become more narrow. Our commute becomes familiar and we stop seeing the new things happening around us. What a challenge this is for billboard designers – how much must their creation stand out before it is noticed?

I noticed the coffee shop on my motorcycle because I had taken a safety class in order to qualify for my license. It was there I learned about the lack of observation skills of every other driver, and how it was important to enhance my own skill. Should all drivers be required to take, and pass, this test?

I recently started taking photos of clouds, skies, sunsets and sunrises. I discovered an interesting phenomenon – the proliferation of man-made objects between us and the sky. With observation, the world is new again! Taking notice of the world around me is an experience I am not giving up soon. You?

Observe.

Miss not a second of your life!

use all your senses

We all know about our five senses. Sight, smell, hearing, taste, touch. We hear about a sixth sense – one of intuition. Non-scientific people propose that we have five subconscious and five psychic senses. Scientific people propose we have a sense of pain, a sense of heat/cold, a sense of balance.

Think about the time you walked into a house, and remarked how it smelled like a memory – maybe, your grandmother's home? How is that explained as a human sense? It certainly is a common occurrence.

However you define an experience like that, the truth is that humans live narrowly in the senses of which they are even aware. We see what we see, we hear what we hear, and so on… Our senses are the way we experience the world. When we use our senses narrowly, our view of the world is narrow.

And our senses are all linked. Taste does not work well without smell. Touch is different without sight. And, we can create our own combinations! Have you ever had someone ask you to describe the flavor of a color? Our life will be richer as we indulge in the sensory perception with which we have been gifted. See the flavor, touch the smell, and hear ALL your senses working.

Use all your senses.

Immerse yourself in the world around you.

have a braincyclone

"Think outside the box" is corporate cliché. If you did think outside the box, there would be no cliché. "Brainstorm" is another overused corporate term. If there were enough molecules active in your fellow workers to engage their brain in stormy activity, there would be no cliché.

Sometimes, prior to starting one of my *Get A Life!* sessions, I subject the audience to beach balls. Everyone knows what to do with beach balls – you throw and bash them to other people in the vicinity. When more attendees arrive, they hear the laughter and see the fun. Immediately their first impression sets a mood for them – one that was unexpected.

So, think outside the box, and when you are asked to problem solve, schedule a "braincyclone" session. The first thing to happen will be a different perspective from all the attendees. When someone attends a "braincyclone" session, they know they are in for a different experience.

Follow that up with a different agenda – one that includes creativity exercises. Follow that up with a different agenda – one that includes creativity exercises. Train of thought whiteboard exercises, acting exercises, improv– …all designed to stir brain molecules and generate. Storm your brains so hard, you create a cyclone!

Have a braincyclone.

Stir the pot just a little – more!

read a new genre

What is your reading pleasure? Sci-fi, mystery, thriller, bestseller? With so many choices, it is easy to find a genre that suits us and stay there. And, like any other rut, our learning and entertainment become narrow.

I never had the opportunity to study Shakespeare during my formal education. When I was in my 30's, I was introduced to Hamlet. I discovered new worlds in the words of the immortal bard. Sure, I needed lots of help, but found that in Tom Stoppard's works and a friend studying for her PhD in literature. My life has been enriched!

Imagine all the other worlds waiting to be discovered in your local bookstore! Or, even in your airport? Next time you are flying, pick up a cheesy romance novel – there is a special section for the cheesiest. As you fly, take care not to laugh at the overuse of words such as 'throbbing' and 'manhood'. By the time you arrive, your flight will have been shorter and you will have been entertained. As you leave, hand the book to your nearest seat mate (who has been wondering about your snickering), and promise them a good time of their own.

Discover new worlds! Embark on amazing adventures! Travel to wondrous destinations! Just move ten feet to your right..

Read a new genre.

Challenge your brain to a new experience!

skip

Count the number of hours you sit on your behind. Count the number of hours you stand in elevators waiting for your floor. Sedentary lifestyles are becoming the norm for many cultures. Personally, I have sat in my car while I banked, ordered food, washed the car.

The trick is to find the motivation to remove sedentary from our life vocabulary. While it does seem to require magic, it simply takes a small amount of discipline, mind control and adjusting our perspective.

The first thing to do is to take a new view of the world around us. Look for opportunities to be active. Park as far from the entrance to the supermarket as possible – ten more minutes of activity. Climb stairs instead of using the elevator – ten more minutes of activity. Use the down escalators to go up – five more minutes of apologizing needlessly to the lazy consumers going in the normal direction! Next time you see a grass path leading to your next destination, detour with skipping – five more minutes of activity.

The second thing to do is conquer fear and insecurity! We have years of conditioning to overcome to allow ourselves to skip in public. People may think you are silly, but you know they are extremely jealous of your freedom!

Skip.

With a friend!

volunteer

One Christmas, I was unable to spend the day with my daughter. Since my day was free, I looked for a place where I could volunteer my time. I discovered that volunteering on Christmas day is booked almost a year ahead. It seems there is a huge desire to show your community spirit – on the one day a year that your peers would notice.

I found a retirement home where I could help with lunch. When I arrived early, they did not know who I was and told me to come back. When I did, I bussed tables, refilled drinks, and generally performed tasks that could have been done by anyone. I was feeling selfishly useless.

At the end of lunch, I was asked to escort a lady to her sister's room. She held my arm, and told me the story of her sister, their life together, and her sister's move into the home. I felt very humble. She then asked why I was there, and I told her my Christmas story. She looked up at me and said, "it is people like you who make the difference."

In that one sentence, my selfishness was squashed. While my humility suffered, I discovered volunteering was not something done to benefit oneself. The rewards go far beyond self glorification.

Volunteer.

You will get more than you ever give!

skulk

I played Thomas Cromwell – Henry VIII's Prime Minister – at two renaissance festivals. In my character research, I discovered he created a spy network, unrivalled in his time, that is the basis for most modern spy networks.

Translating this to a believable villain, and one that everyone loves to hate, was challenging. I found the best character reference for spying was the Pink Panther, and turned this into an event of its own – I used the word 'skulk' to describe it.

Imagine being able to gather a half dozen patrons in a line, teach them the basics of skulking, and have them follow you in a Cromwell conga. What power! What entertainment for those watching!

With kids, skulking was a completely difference experience. They believed we could disappear from view while skulking and reappear in a new location – fooling the audience. Their ability to suspend disbelief was an inspiration. I teach skulking in my Get A Life! sessions, and there are always mixed responses. Mostly, though, the participants feel a childlike sense of freedom, without the usual fear and insecurities of silliness.

Skulk.

It is always "inappropriate"!

men and women = different

Ask your partner for advice, and this is what you might hear:

> Girl: *"If I were you, I would go home."*

> Boy: *"Go home."*

Certainly, these are stereotypical responses, however they do tell us something about the differences between men and women. In this particular case, Girl is empathetic – offering a solution in a gentle means. Boy's solution is also offered – albeit in a more direct manner.

Belonging to one of these categories, I find communication is key to any relationship. I have a close male friend with whom I have worked for many years. People around us have remarked how they do not understand our conversations – we seem to know what the other is thinking, and we seem to finish each other's sentences. Without knowing it, we subconsciously appreciate how each other thinks.

Finding how to do that with people who are not close to you requires more effort. If you understand that the first reaction of Girl may be to empathize, and the first reaction of Boy may be to solve – regardless of the existence of any 'problem', you can make great steps in managing relationships with people.

People!

Celebrate your differences..

get real

Back in the 19th century, some (now) famous writers created some interesting fiction. It was science, but not any science imagined by the world. Science fiction was born.

The next step was the introduction of threats from worlds of which we could only imagine, and UFOs and aliens were invented. From those auspicious beginnings, the world is now full of perceived UFOs and aliens. People have been abducted and have alien implants. Aliens walk among us and even run countries!

Surely, an invention of writers can hardly be reality? Yet, many people believe that aliens exist and have interacted with humans. While the cosmos is revealing more of its mysteries every year, alien life is not one that actual astronomers can prove.

Humans are so gullible when it comes to a convincing story, and few of us actually do our own research – instead, preferring to be convinced by non-scientific people without actual proof.

The public is subjected to lies and conjecture in so many ways. Do you believe because you are told it is so? Take it upon yourself to believe that which is proven, and read the rest as fiction.

Get real.

Belief is a personal thing!

try a new salad dressing

Pinch your nostrils together with your fingers. Now, say the word "Ranch" as nasally as you can. This is how the American dining experience sounds to me. When ordering salad, the majority of diners with whom I eat, order Ranch salad dressing.

I think I know the reason for the popularity of Ranch. I once tried Blue Cheese… I switched back to Ranch rather quickly. Ranch is the safe option. Mild, pleasing to the palate, does not assault the senses, adds flavor – who would choose anything else?

Of course, this is a parallel to our lives. For the most part, we select the safe choice. Take bungee jumping for example. We have heard about the 'dangers' of bungee – at least, we have heard all the sensationalist news. Did you hear about the regulations placed on bungee, and the reductions in accidents since then?

Given a chance to bungee, we snort and refuse. "Surely you would not expect me to take that chance??" Yet, the adventure is safe, and the experience adds depth to your life.

Take the Ranch challenge – try a new spicy, tasty, flavorful, adventurous change to your dinner experience. Now, do that in your life!

Try a new salad dressing.

Confuse your date!

have defining momentS

Once upon a time, I managed to shove my hand through a glass pane in a door. The end result was 40 stitches, and some weeks of healing. It allowed me to reflect on my life up to that moment – and then beyond, and I realized it was a turning point. For me, this was a defining moment in my life.

For some people, there is some major event in their life that is their own 'defining moment'. It is the pivot point where their life before and life after have changed substantially.

And while it is an incredible experience to be blessed with this single realization, I have discovered that there are so many moments in my life that help define me. After one of my *Get A Life!* sessions, an 82-year-old attendee told me that the session was something they needed every day of their life. From this amazing moment, my approach to my session changed substantially. It became another of the defining momentS of my life.

Recognize the moments where your life is redefined. It may not be apparent immediately – in fact, it is more often retrospective recognition. Be amazed that your life has been spun in a new positive direction. Understand the impact of that moment, and by virtue of being able to identify them, have more!

Have defining moments.

One is not enough!

never make the same mistake twice... always invent new ones

I am often accused of being too smart for my own boots and never making a mistake. While it may be my visible ego that exposes this perception, it is simply not true. Maybe the perception is such because I cover up my mistakes well? Or, because I do not repeat my mistakes?

One of the biggest compliments I have received in my life was that I was a sponge – my desire to fill my head with information was only surpassed by the space I have in my head to store that information. Since curiosity is a key for me, it seems such a waste to repeat a mistake – there is not enough time to learn something more than once.

Human nature, of course, intervenes. Remembering all our mistakes and their lessons is a daunting task. Learning from other people's mistakes is even more difficult. While we stand back and watch someone else crash, we are full of advice to correct and repair their mishap. Put us in the exact same situation, and we reproduce their experience!

My favorite approach to life is to blunder. Keep your curiosity raging, repeat nobody's mistakes, and learn, learn, learn.

Never repeat a mistake.

You will get blamed for the first one, too!

learn something new every day

Our entry to this world is naked and hungry. Our eventual exit is expected to be the same. What is it that we fill our life with?

I marvel in the days I have on this planet. On a regular basis, stop, take a look around you. Wherever you are, there is something amazing within your sight. One hundred years ago, the concept of transportation as it is today was unthinkable. Going to a movie to watch the efforts of many people to produce 90 minutes or so of entertainment was science fiction.

How did we get all of these modern conveniences? What is the origin of electricity? How is chocolate made? The secrets of the universe are being revealed to us with each decade – and with every new cable television channel.

The first character I played at a renaissance festival was the Earl of Surrey, who lived in the 16th century. By the age of nineteen, he had commanded battalions in war, understood five languages fluently, translated Virgil's epic poem 'The Aeneid' into English, introduced iambic pentameter to Britain, and much more. Four hundred years later, the Earl would have been lost in the information available at his fingertips. Yet, even learning something new every day, I have a long way to catch him!

Learn something new every day.

There are less than there were yesterday!

act

Growing up, my mother told me to always tell the truth. What she forgot to enlighten me of was 'tact'. With said skill missing from my repertoire, I was able to test some of my emotions on a regular basis. Especially when bullies sent their little brothers to smack me.

Skip forward 20 years, and now the defenses of 'silliness' I employed for so long have been put to good use in street theater. Playing a strong character with a reputation of being a bastard was a stretch, I promise! And then, playing an over excitable, retentive accountant with a hobby of measuring things was the complete opposite.

Acting provides a vehicle to put yourself in the shoes of other people. You learn a lot about individual character traits, and by exaggeration of your own version of their passion, emotions and foibles, you learn a lot about yourself.

Acting classes teach you how to understand and express emotion. While the majority do not purposely seek to improve you, this is an end result. With permission to explore emotion using a character as the agent, you learn more about your own feelings and reactions to situations. When you face the real world, you are now armed.

Act.

Get in touch with your emotions!

unleash the genie

In fairy tales, there is talk of a magic lamp. Rub it, and a genie shall appear to grant you three wishes. While this may be a nice dream, it is more fantasy than winning a lottery.

However, there is a genie inside each of us. It can perform magical things to amaze and surprise. The genie knows who we are, and has special skills that need to be unleashed. Identifying the genie is, often, the most difficult part.

I have a friend in her 30's who discovered a long lost aptitude for playing the piano. She started with an electronic keyboard, set time aside in her life, scheduled lessons, and unleashed the genie. Within 18 months, she was playing at her local church on regular weekends.

Another friend discovered her sewing skills were more than run of the mill. While holding a steady job, she began sewing costumes for her local renaissance festival performers. Eventually she was commissioned to create major costume experiences for the owner of the festival.

What is your passion? Where is your genie hiding? Tempt your genie by trying new skills, until eventually, the genie cannot resist!

Unleash the genie.

Give yourself power over your dreams!

if everything takes longer than you think...
think longer!

Planning for any activity is a science. It requires intimate knowledge of the task at hand, understanding of the necessary skill set, a recognition of the players involved, access to appropriate resources and your own management and communication skills.

It would seem that after each activity is complete, planning would be easier. Comparing past results to their plan would reveal overruns, identify barriers to completion, and measure the performance of the participants. The next plan would take into account this review, and over time, planning would become more accurate.

Human nature, apparently, intervenes and provides excuses for us to ignore the lessons we have learned and repeat our mistakes. The number of projects we hear about that come in on time or under budget is relatively small – whether a government or personal project.

There are two ways to ensure your activity plans are more accurate. First, spend more time on the plan. Factor in reviews of past successes or failures – yours or not. Second, if all your activities have taken longer than your past estimates, increase your estimates!

Think longer.

Think longer.

choose well

Living in our past is an easy way to stop growing. It provides many excuses for our inability to become a whole person. And, it allows us to blame other people for decisions we have made.

In order to accept who we are, and believe that we are whole and complete, we must accept our past. Part of that is accepting all the decisions we have made. While some of them are mistakes, if we continue to lament them, or regret them, we will not be able to move forward in our lives.

While a choice you made in the past was bad – then, you must accept this choice as the best you could make, with the information you had, in the emotional state you were in, at the time it happened. Knowing the result enables you to never make that decision again – and instills in you the capacity to make better choices in your future.

Instead of saying "if I could do it over again", you must know that under those circumstances, you would make the same decision. Now you know the result, recognize it as a turning point, repair damage, learn the lesson, and make wiser choices in your future. And next time, remove your emotions from the important life decisions.

Choose well.

Stand by your decisions!

in purity, there is no justification

In a recent argument with a relative, I uncovered something unnerving. For every question I asked, there were no answers – simply a defense.
I tried hard to elicit answers to my questions, and it became emotionally difficult very quickly.

I stepped back in an attempt to understand the dynamics of the situation, and realized I was not qualified to be a psychiatrist. But I did understand that my relative was hiding something. They claimed their motives were pure, but the end result did not appear – on the outside – to be anything but selfish. Their continued justification of their motives was simply not believable.

I find that one of the joys in my life is being able to do something for someone else. The more anonymous, the better – for me. If someone benefits from an action of mine, that is reward enough for me. I do not need to seek recognition or reward, and I strive to maintain those motives in all that I do.

If your heart is true and your motives are pure, there is no need to spend any of your time providing justification for your actions.

Justify nothing.

Be pure of heart!

create idiot vacuums

Driving on a packed highway is one of life's amazing experiences. It can turn a normally sane adult into a complete idiot. Studies have been done showing that if everyone kept two car lengths from each other, there would be no such thing as traffic jams. But, WE know the truth — you leave as little as half a car length and some idiot will take that space.

Take a different perspective and play the "idiot vacuum" game on your commute to work. Purposely create a space in front of you that looks inviting and watch while some idiot is sucked right into it!

These spaces are "idiot vacuums". You get 2 points for every idiot that is sucked in. You lose 1 point if they escape to someone else's idiot vacuum before you have a chance to create another and suck another idiot into your game.

When you get to the office, compare your point score with your fellow workers. Post them to a prominent bulletin board at your office. Don't cheat — you need accurate numbers to plot "idiot vacuum" trends. Imagine how your commute will improve!

Create idiot vacuums.

They won't know, and you will feel better.

rock your own world

I have a lot of single friends who complain about not having a significant other. They spend much time lamenting the lack of partner, and much time waiting for someone to have an impact on their life. When you read their personal ads, they find they want someone to "rock their world".

One of them in particular spent a lot of time arguing with people who suggested that they find themselves first. They claimed to be whole as they were, but it was obvious they thought they still had a hole. For most people, it is easy to claim the lack of someone else in their life as the reason for their unhappiness.

Whatever psychobabble it is, I have experienced the concept of becoming whole. I have discovered that happiness truly does come from within, and truly is your own responsibility. The result is improved relationships with everyone in your life, less time spent whining and more time getting on with your life.

It does, however, require that you find that happiness. You must know your joy list. You must smile – often. You must know what brings 'happy' to your life, and you must indulge in 'happy' – regularly. Look! Your happiness is right there in front of you...

Rock your own world.

Stop waiting for someone else to drive!

adjust your perspective

Lie on your back in a grassy field on a sunny day and watch the clouds. Look! There is an elephant... Now a rabbit! Stay there into the night and look into the moon! From the northern hemisphere, you will clearly see the 'man in the moon'. From the southern hemisphere, it is a rabbit family watching TV.

Perspective has a lot to do with the ability of your imagination to think beyond the normal daily grind. When you see a lit sign that says 'Wells argo", do you think of it simply as a blown light bulb? Or, do you ask who knocked the "F" out of the sign?

Perspective has a lot to do with where you are located. Standing close to something, you will see it differently than when you stand at a distance. Move to the left or right a little for another view. Do you change your location to see with a different eye, or are you stuck in the same place with the same sights?

Perspective has a lot to do with the things you know. Your opinions, your beliefs, your viewpoint are all tailored by your education and upbringing. Understanding requires you to learn, not just read about things in newspapers or hear about them on TV. Put on some different colored glasses and change the way you see the world.

Adjust your perspective.

Does it really look like that?!

feed your imagination

For most people, variety is a different flavor of ice cream. Their habits become their comfort zone, and there seems to be little desire to change. Certainly, there are people for whom this is acceptable. And that would be a separate book!

Feeding and exercising your imagination is a conduit to variety and growth in your life. If you think life is the time spent accumulating assets in a race against the rest of the consumer population, your imagination is dulled.

Sure, there are people who claim that watching *The Simpsons* provides imagination food. Wrapping college humor in a cartoon does not make it any more imaginative.

To truly exercise your imagination, you need to branch out. Read a new genre. Try a new salad dressing. Change the station on your radio. Wear red Converse sneakers. Watch TV that is not simply escapism. Travel. Draw. Paint. Write. Visit renaissance festivals and watch the glass blowing exhibits. Take ballroom dancing lessons. Learn acting. Make movies. Eat frog legs.

Discover what makes your imagination hungry and spend time feeding it.

Feed your imagination.

It is getting hungry!

imagine the impossible

What if Galileo accepted everything around him, and never imagined the impossible? How about Einstein? What if Edison had accepted his first failure and not tried that extra thousand times to succeed? Our world would be a much different place!

Most success in our life comes after looking at the task ahead, then planning and executing well. Underlying the result is our confidence that we can complete the task and achieve success. Many tasks in our lives are not attempted, due to our lack of that confidence.

Would you try something if there was a guarantee of success? What if you were able to minimize the risk, so that even a negative result would be acceptable? How about if there were no guarantee of success, but the result would change the world?

Often, what we think is impossible is not. We may lack the education, knowledge or contacts necessary to achieve success. We may not know that a few preparatory tasks would reduce the complexity and cause success.

Sticking that first toe into the water can be less daunting if you can conceive success – believe that the end is possible, imagine the impossible, imagine your success, and dive in.

Imagine the impossible.

Imagine when the impossible happens!

be childlike

After one of the first times I had audience members skulk with me in a *Get A Life!* session, one of the participants told me that it felt like they were six again. They expressed elation at the experience.

I have since discovered that skulking in front of an audience is not a threatening experience – for most people. And it allows us to play for a moment and explore the child within.

This is completely different from the behavior of some of my coworkers. Volunteer organizations can be like going back to high school. Petty jealousies, gossip, backstabbing, lies, thievery, bullying, whining… if it is a childish behavior, it thrives. In the business world, it has its own name: *politics*.

There is a gap between childish and childlike behavior. Childlike is play, childish is not acceptable – in children nor adults. The fine line is being able to engage in childlike behavior – when appropriate, without it becoming childish.

Being able to distinguish is difficult for some people who have not seen their inner child in a long time. Their negativity should not prevent you from adding this balance to your life and your work.

Be childlike.

Let your suppressed child play!

give your heart

A friend of mine was having a difficult breakup with a boyfriend. I was wearing a Celtic heart necklace, so I gave it to her with this thought – while she was wearing it, she would have love with her always. She told me later, that such a small motif had made a huge difference.

After I told this story to end one of my *Get A Life!* sessions, a lady in the audience approached me with thanks. She had been having trouble reaching her daughter, but my session had given her some new perspectives and new ways she could try to reach her daughter. I had a small red heart stone in my pocket, and I gave it to her.

Later, she sent me an email to tell me that when she arrived home, she asked her daughter how important it was to know that her mother loved her. Her daughter told her it was very important. She gave her daughter the heart, and told her that every time she saw it, she would know her mother loved her. Since then, it was never out of sight, and she told me it had made a huge difference.

Keep a heart with you, and you will have love, wherever you go.

Give someone your heart.

It makes a huge difference.

Get A Life!

Get A Life! is a simple axiom. It is about balancing your work and your life, and being able to put more life in your work. It is about wallowing in the child in you. It is about play and the permission to play. And, it is about the freedom and quality of your life.

There are many paths – the one that suits you is not one that suits anyone else. Your path needs to be selected and tailored by you – with passion and conscious positive choice.

The steps outlined here are simply those that suit me the best. While they might assist in guiding your path, it is your interpretation and spin that will let these add value to your life.

1 Check your **I-Sight**
   Take a new look at everything around you.

2 Learn new **I-Talents**
   Exercise all the skills you never knew you had!

3 Use your **I-magination**
   Think impossible things in new ways.

4 Have an **I-Wanna** list
   Keep a list of everything you always wanted to do.

5 Take some **I-Drops**
   Discover new ways to improve your perspective.

Get A Life!

Find your balance.

be extraordinary

Each of us is the sum of our own experiences.
This unique package of who we are is not repeated
anywhere on the planet. While we may have a
doppelganger or two wandering around, their life is
not the same package.

And in the midst of the normality of our lives, we
often find ourselves being treated as though we were
just another human being on the planet. It is
imperative to maintain a sense of ourselves, a sense
of wholeness, and a sense of importance in the face
of all that is ordinary.

To remind ourselves of our selves, write down this
mnemonic:

IMXO

It represents "**I** a**M** e**X**tra**O**rdinary" and can serve as
a trigger when we are feeling disrespected, or treated
like sheeple.

Simply knowing that we are extraordinary can add a
level of confidence to our lives. No longer will we
require approval from anyone else to be ourselves.
No longer will we seek out acceptance from others
in order to continue living according to their 'rules'.

All it takes, is for you to recognize and believe in
yourself, to believe in the power of you and all that
you can achieve. **URXO**!

Be extraordinary.

yoU aRe eXtra-Ordinary!

thanks to...

Bob, for major inspiration. Thanks for helping me see in new ways. Your light shines long after your presence has been felt.

Alison, for reviewing everything. Thanks for keeping me straight and telling me I was nearly done after every review.

Kelly, for long term literary guidance. Thanks for your constant doses of reality.

Elizabeth, for editing and encouragement.

Mandi, for editing perfectly and correctly.

Ilena, Shelley and Ivy, for reviews.

Wendy and John, for new connections, new laughter, and new lives.

Sawyer, for being my friend.